How to Milk the Cash Cow

Taking a vacant, city, single family home and "utterly" turning it into a money making machine

By Rhonda Graham

Warning: It is illegal to reproduce or distribute this copyrighted work. Criminal copyright infringement, including but not limited to, infringement without monetary gain is investigated by the FBI and is punishable by five years in Federal Prison and fines up to $250,000.00.

ISBN: 978-1475107463

Published by:

My Manager, LLC

5513 William Flynn Highway, Suite 400-322,

Gibsonia, PA 15044

Mymanager0007@gmail.com

Copyright © 2012 My Manager, LLC

For more copies of this book, please visit:

www.howtomilkthecashcow.com

This book is dedicated in memory of our friend Matt Scott

CONTENTS

Foreword 11

Getting Started 17

Getting your house ready to rent rooms 19
Fix the house up using very little money 19
Convert the bedrooms into rooms for rent 19
Prepare each bedroom for a room for rent 20
Living room space may be required 21
Get the kitchen ready 21
A touchpad key-code entry for the main door 22

Set up the utilities 24
Standard utilities 24
Cable television and wireless internet 24
Call the local gas provider 25
Land-line phone 25
Sewage and Water 26
Laundry 27
Garbage/recycling pick-up 27

Why all the amenities? 29
Offering more than your competitors 29
Make it hard for residents to leave 30
You want to give them their best option for housing 30
Because it works so well 31

Filling your property with a resident 33

Finding your resident 35
   Place an ad in the local newspaper 35
   Housing assistance agencies and charity organizations 35
   Word of Mouth 36
   Waiting list 37

Who is your potential tenant? 38
   Someone looking for convenience and affordability 38
   Single, divorced, or parents wanting to live closer to their children 38
   College students 39
   All male/female residents 40

Making Appointments 41
   Questions you may want to ask your potential resident: 41
   Questions they may ask you: 41
   Scheduling a time to see the home and the room 45
   It's Milkin' time: Making Appointments 47

Showing the home and the room 49
   How long should it take? 49
   Show them around the home 49
   What to do if they are interested 50
   What if they are not interested? 51

What you need to fill the room 52
   A completed application and processing fee 52
   A qualified resident 53
   Picture of resident 53
   A deposit to hold the room 54
   The first week's rent 54
   Paying ahead on rent 55

Strategies for filling rooms quickly 56
    Take your time answering questions 56
    Show them around 56
    Bulk your appointments together 58
    How "in demand" are these rooms? 59
    It's Milkin' Time: Filling Your Room 60

The Application Process 63

The Application Process 65
    Where do you get applications? 65
    How does the potential tenant get an application? 65
    What do you do with the application? 66
    Background check 67
    Credit check 67
    Criminal background research 68

The Super-Tenant 69

The Super-Tenant 71
    What is a super-tenant? 71
    How do you find a super-tenant? 72
    How do you compensate a super-tenant? 73

Now That You Have a Qualified Resident, What is Next? 75

Now you have a qualified resident. What is next? 77
    Let them know they are approved to move in 77
    What you should let them know up front 77
    Give them a receipt for payment 78
    Statement of account 78

What do new residents need from you? 80

    A copy of the house rules 80
    A key for their room 81
    Key code for the front door 81
    Month to month verbal lease agreement 81

Setting up proper communications 83
    Emergency numbers 83
    How will your resident contact you? 83
    How will you contact your resident? 84
    Providing a land line phone 85

Making sure the property is properly maintained 89
    Do it yourself or hire help 89
    How do you know what needs to be done? 89

Cleaning the common areas 91
    Cleaning the common area 91
    Suggestions on the cost of cleaning 93
    Its Milking time: Cleaning Personnel 94

Maintain good records 96
    Good record keeping 96

Monitor utility abuse 97
    Heating 97
    Central air or air conditioners 97
    Water usage 97
    It's Milkin' Time: Utility Abuse 98

Keeping your residents living in your home 103
    Create a good environment 103
    Be prepared when vacancy arises 103
    Creative attention to residents 104
    Keep property maintained properly 104
    Screen potential residents well 105

Moving a resident out 106
    Receive a notice to move out 106
    Criteria for refunding a deposit 106
    Refunding a deposit 107
    When not to refund a deposit 107

Physical removal of a resident and their property 108
    Creative evictions 108
    It's Milkin time: Security Deposit 109

Locking out a resident 111
    24-hour lockout notice 111
    Deleting the key code to main entry 111
    Change out the landlord locks 112

Rules Violations and house rules 114
    What are rules violations? 114
    What are house rules? 115
    It's Milkin' Time: Rules Violations 116

Other policies to consider when renting to residents 121
    Being responsible for tenant's property 121
    Suggest a renter's insurance policy per resident 121
    Smoking policy for residents 122
    Linens and reusable items 122

Glossary 123

Glossary 125

Index 129

Foreword

In 2002, my husband and I set out on an adventure in real estate investing. We had no experience, but we were reading a lot of investing material and found a book that guided us to a class on how to find homes that we could acquire using a lease purchase agreement from owners. We would turn them around and rent them out to families that qualified for a rent-to-own program we created for the homes. It was a sound idea and worked out really well.

We got our first home lined up and I remember being extremely nervous and hoping we did everything the way we were supposed to. The second one was easier and so on. We slowly built up our property base and it was working out very nicely. After a while, we learned that if the residents got behind on rent or once a family moved out, it took a few months to fill the home back up with a qualified family. We required that they had money down. We let them make payments on this down payment and several times we never did get the complete down payment. It would cost us to carry the mortgage and all the utilities. It was quite burdensome and we discovered that all of our profits were soon eaten up in a matter of a few months. What was even worse was if we had two homes or more that were vacant we were losing out tremendously.

After a few months of having one vacancy, my husband, Chris' sister mentioned that we should try doing what her friend Matt, who we used to have work with us, does; which was renting out rooms in a building. We were curious, but also very cautious. After thinking about it for some time, we decided the idea may have some validity. Chris decided to meet with Matt and find out more.

He explained what he did and showed Chris the lease he used for his residents and he also showed him a property that was already set up and renting out rooms and they shared a common area. We really loved the idea after we learned more because we learned that if one resident doesn't pay, you still have the other residents paying you so you are not scrambling to find money to pay your house payment. This could really resolve that issue for us. And the more we thought about it, we discovered that it could be very profitable.

We had a vacant property and we went to work right away. Instantly, it was productive and we had a wait list of people that wanted a room. To be quite frank with you, we could not wait for one of our other homes to become vacant so we could use it to create shared housing for our new found hopeful residents.

We now have many of these homes and we have fine-tuned the service of renting rooms out.

This book was created as a guide to those of you that may be suffering with paying two or more mortgages, painstakingly dealing with residents that are always late with payments, or just looking to take a city home and turn it into an investment that requires very little work and gets you an immediate return. You may be a landlord that is looking for an easier way that is far more lucrative. Perhaps you are someone that is dealing with a possible foreclosure and you do not want to lose your house or your credit. These times can be scary!

We all need a good idea to come along once in a while. I hope you walk away from reading this with a new hope! You can take your home and with very little effort, turn your financial situation around. These are very creative ideas that were inspired by trial and error, insight, intuition and experience. This is what my husband and I do in our investing careers and I hope by sharing these ideas with enough people, in our own little way, we can make the world a better place. ~ Rhonda Graham

Getting Started

GETTING YOUR HOUSE READY TO RENT ROOMS

FIX THE HOUSE UP USING VERY LITTLE MONEY
It will save you money if you can do the work of getting rooms ready in your vacant house by yourself. What you have to do will depend on what condition your house is in. Whether your house is small or big will not matter. You don't want to put a ton of cash into it; you want to get a ton of cash out!

If you can't do the work yourself, you might want to think about hiring a basic carpenter to do some minor work on a couple areas to get your home ready.

CONVERT THE BEDROOMS INTO ROOMS FOR RENT
First of all, all bedrooms need to have a door and a keyed entry lock. Next, you want to take any rooms in the house that can be converted into a bedroom (living

rooms, dining rooms, family room) and prepare those rooms as well. You can rent out the bedrooms that are already completed to help pay for the cost. Keep construction very simple. If you are converting one of those rooms into a room for rent, you will need to partition off the room with a temporary wall and a door with a lock and key entry to secure that bedroom. False walls are ideal for this purpose and are described at:

http://www.ehow.com/how_6572513_build-false-wall.html

PREPARE EACH BEDROOM FOR A ROOM FOR RENT
Each bedroom gets a bed, dresser, fire alarm, and lock-and-key entry to guarantee privacy. There are companies that have locks that are interchangeable. All you have to do is use a master key and remove the entire lock. It is only the size of a spark plug and it slides into the door knob. It comes out of the door knob and the door

knob stays intact. They can be removed in a matter of seconds. Make copies of your keys to give to your residents. You are able to change out the key so that if the current tenant moves out, you can provide the new tenant with a different lock and key.

LIVING ROOM SPACE MAY BE REQUIRED

Ask a local Building Code Enforcement Officer to see what space is required for how many rooms you will be renting. In a living room you may want to add a used couch from a thrift store, a few pictures and lamps, and a television on a small stand for comfort and entertainment. It is not required but can be a nice selling point. This will also be a great place to post your information for all residents to see, like the house rules.

GET THE KITCHEN READY

Provide appliances in the kitchen for the resident's comfort and convenience. Try to search yard sales for basic dishes and pans. Whatever you would imagine you need to go camping would be a good item for a kitchen in this type of home. Some basic silverware, plates, cups, bowls, pots and pans will do. Add a washer and dryer to the kitchen area for convenience instead of in a laundry room or basement. Repair any cupboards that need fixing. Please do not forget your fire extinguisher and fire alarms.

A TOUCHPAD KEY-CODE ENTRY FOR THE MAIN DOOR

You might choose to control the resident's entry into the home with a digital key code. Each resident is assigned a four digit number in which they punch into the touch-pad on the deadbolt for the door to get in. Use a number that is easy for them to remember like the last four digits of their social security number. This is something easy for us to record and attach to their file. The door automatically locks after they enter and they don't need a card or key to get in which keeps them safe and secure. The digital key pad lock can hold up to 20 numbers at any given time with endless combinations to enter. If you need to change a key code for a resident, it only takes seconds. Assign a different key code for your cleaning person, your maintenance manager, and even yourself.

Set up the Utilities

Standard utilities

If it is not already done, you need to set up all the utilities. Call and have the electric and gas utilities turned on, the water service started, and make sure that the sewage bill is paid. These are primary utilities that need to be established in order to prepare the home.

Cable television and wireless internet

Because you may want to include cable and wireless internet, be prepared to start them up and get installation in place. Call the cable company and ask them how long it takes to set up and have a plan in place. Some companies have the cable television, wireless internet, as well as a land line phone put together and there is only one bill every month. When the cable company comes, have them put a cable outlet in every room that you will rent. It is an added expense, but it is a one-time cost that pays off. Residents all seem to want cable and love the option of wireless internet.

CALL THE LOCAL GAS PROVIDER
This will provide heat and possibly run the stove, water heater, washer and/or dryer. Some companies may provide a budget plan where you pay the same amount every month unless the bill gets extremely high. Monitor any abuse and you should have a manageable bill.

LAND-LINE PHONE
Find out about getting a land-line phone and how long it takes to get installed. Offer only one phone that is hard-wired into the home, located in the common area. For you, as the homeowner, this ensures that you can reach the tenants and you can possibly arrange to leave messages for each individual if necessary without going out of

the budgeted amount for your bill. You may be able to work with your local phone company about blocking all outgoing calls to phone hotlines and calls that can rack up a bill. The phone company should be able to set up where your residents may only call local and free long-distance calls.

SEWAGE AND WATER

These are primary utilities that you should already be used to paying if you are the homeowner. Because of varying usage, water may fluctuate slightly, but should be around the same amount every month once you have all residents living in the home. Sewage should be a budget-able amount every month. Keep the sewage bill paid. If you don't pay your bill, guess how they shut off the sewage? They turn off your water. Now you have two big problems. Both sewage and water will require a fee to be turned back on.

Laundry

This isn't a utility but something you may want to provide for all your homes as you may also find this as important as any utility. It is fantastic for residents when they are able to have on-site laundry. Guaranteed; it can be the deal maker many times. You can usually find a washer and/or dryer in the local paper or on a local free online site that is relatively inexpensive and quickly. It is not a huge expense and it is well received by your residents. Offering laundry facilities will probably give your service the edge over all other competitors.

Garbage/Recycling Pick-up

Set up the garbage service to be picked up once a week. It is very affordable for what you get. You just have to make sure it is out on the curb by the evening before pick-up. You can have a weekly cleaning person who comes in and picks up all the garbage, replaces the bags, and puts the garbage out by the curb.

WHY ALL THE AMENITIES?

OFFERING MORE THAN YOUR COMPETITORS

How do you know you are giving more? You need to study your competitors within your area and just give a little more (like laundry) for a little less (a lower price) than they do and you have the edge. Look in the local paper under rooms-for-rent in your area and give them a call to see exactly what they offer. You can adopt some pretty good ideas of what you can do and perhaps what not to do. This helps you with a few things:

1. It helps you to know who your competitors are and how to price your rooms for rent.

2. It helps you to figure out what exactly you can do more of and possibly offer it to your residents.

MAKE IT HARD FOR RESIDENTS TO LEAVE

You want to make sure that you are not only offering more than the competitor, but also making it very hard for a tenant to leave because it is so convenient. It is more cost effective to keep someone in place than to keep replacing poor residents. They do not have to come up with an electric company start-up fee. They do not have to deal with vendors for garbage and sewage, cable, internet, or electric. All of those expenses are handled by you or a "super-tenant" (covered in a later chapter). They just need to come up with a very affordable weekly rent.

YOU WANT TO GIVE THEM THEIR BEST OPTION FOR HOUSING

Offer a lock and key entry into their own room equipped with a bed and a dresser. They also get access to the kitchen, living room, and bathroom. You are possibly providing all utilities such as water, sewage, garbage, cable, wireless internet access, and on-site complementary laundry. You are offering them a convenient, safe place to stay at a reasonable rate.

BECAUSE IT WORKS SO WELL

Don't forget, every time you fill a room for a month, they are helping you pay the mortgage, the utilities, any expenses to keep up with the home, and putting money in your pocket. Also, you are giving residents a safe, affordable place to live with everything that they will need. You are giving your community a housing option to some of its citizens. It is a win-win for everyone.

Filling your property with a resident

FINDING YOUR RESIDENT

PLACE AN AD IN THE LOCAL NEWSPAPER

In order to find good residents, you can place an ad in the local newspaper. This ad may read, "ROOM For Rent. Centrally located, $xx.00/week includes all utilities, cable & internet. Call (your number) or email (your email address). An ad may cost you so much a month to have it run continually, but it will consistently prove to pay off to fill your property with good residents. Generally, an ad like this should bring you about 1-2 calls a day with interested residents from a paper with a circulation of about 35,000. Just keep your ad running in the paper until you have the residents moved in.

HOUSING ASSISTANCE AGENCIES AND CHARITY ORGANIZATIONS

Another way of filling properties is working with great organizations that help to find housing for people. Write a letter to each and every organization that is established in your area that works specifically in helping the community find housing for people. Give them all the details of your "rooms for rent" and offer them your contact information. You can partner alongside great organizations that are glad to have a place that is safe, reliable, and affordable to help place anyone in need. You will love it because they give you vouchers for the amount of rent that each individual qualifies for. If you build yourself a good reputation and help these terrific organizations who help others, you may find yourself an excellent resource for filling your property with terrific residents.

WORD OF MOUTH

When you are established, residents will tell others about your rooms. Keep a good reputation by offering a great place to stay for a reasonable rate and the word will get around. After sustaining a good living environment and when you have residents that need to move, the residents still living in the home may have someone they know that wants to move in. They may turn out to be a good qualified resident.

Waiting list

You may also want to maintain a waiting list for the rooms. After all of your rooms are filled with a resident, you may still get interested people who would like to have a room for rent. Compile a list of these interested people referred to as your "waiting list". They are waiting for a room. Taken by the order in which they called, call them back when you have a vacancy. You never know when you are going to get a person who needs to move out of your home right away. Keeping a waiting list may give you a new resident without having to place a fresh ad in the newspaper with additional cost.

WHO IS YOUR POTENTIAL TENANT?

SOMEONE LOOKING FOR CONVENIENCE AND AFFORDABILITY

If you can offer them a place to stay that is affordable, offers the conveniences of modern living and the simplicity of a weekly all-inclusive rent, you have something great to offer. If your house is located in an area that provides public transportation, this may be something they may be looking for. Some of your potential tenants may not be able to drive. They may also want the convenience of having stores, work, or friends nearby.

SINGLE, DIVORCED, OR PARENTS WANTING TO LIVE CLOSER TO THEIR CHILDREN

Some of the time, the people who apply for the rooms-for-rent may be single and have left home and are looking for a place to be on their own. It may be a person starting over after a divorce or poor relationship and wants a place to stay that is convenient. They may want no obligation to a long lease or setting up utilities of their own. Others just do not want to bother with a mortgage or rent with all the added expenses of utilities. You may have a parent who wants to live closer to their children and do not want to impose on them by moving in with them. This will give them the convenience of getting to visit their children or grandchildren who are now close by.

COLLEGE STUDENTS
Depending on location, they may be a college student. College students love the low cost, wireless internet, and the freedom to come and go as they please. They don't have to look for furniture or kitchen utensils for a new apartment. All of that is already supplied for them. You offer convenience and affordability which is just what they are looking for.

All male/female residents

Another idea is having all male/female residents. There may be requests for it and it does work out nicely when you work alongside agencies that want to provide shelters for woman who are trying to relocate due to domestic violence. When the agency needs housing for someone, you can have a professional case worker who calls you and has screened the tenant for you. Working with these agencies is very rewarding and you are also providing a valuable community service.

Making Appointments

Questions you may want to ask your potential resident:

- What exactly are you hoping to find?

- How long are you looking to rent?

- How did you find out about us?

The rest of the conversation usually leads back to you answering questions about how things are set up, what they will owe, and how soon they can move in.

Questions they may ask you:
A lot of the time they have many questions. Here are some of the most common questions and some potential answers you may find useful:

Do I have to share a bathroom?

Yes, all residents share the bathroom (unless the room has its own private one).

Do you have laundry?

Laundry is included and it is set up in a convenient location.

Do I get a television?

No, you must provide your own. There is a cable hookup placed in each bedroom.

Is there a long lease?

No, there is a verbal month-to-month lease. You only need to give a one-week notice if you are moving.

Do I have to give a security deposit?

Yes, one week's total rent is the deposit. It is refundable. In order to get your deposit back you must provide one week's notice before leaving. It does not have to be written but confirmed by the homeowner. You also have to return the room in good condition, as well as give the key back upon the move-out date and have all rent paid in full.

Can someone else live with me?

Because it is a fire hazard, we are not permitted by our insurance company to have more than one adult per room. If they would like to rent a second room as well, perhaps we can set up an appointment for them. However, you are permitted guests.

Can I bring my dog/cat?

Sorry, pets are not permitted. (If you do decide to have pets, realize there can be extensive damage as well as an odor problem. Having considered these things and still decide to have pets, you will have to let every resident, not just one and this can get out-of-hand pretty quickly, but it's your call. If you do, I would recommend a deposit for each individual pet and additional house rules which you will have to create).

Can I pay in advance?

Absolutely. Whichever is more convenient for you to pay - by the month or longer or weekly if you prefer.

I know that I want it, can I just move in?

Sure, let's set up an appointment for you to see the room, to gather information for your application to run a background check and get this started right now. (Still put them through the same process as everyone else. Until you have money in hand, a resident that is approved, and the resident moved in, nothing is guaranteed)

SCHEDULING A TIME TO SEE THE HOME AND THE ROOM

Generally, if they seem genuinely interested, try to make the appointment for the resident to see the home quickly, the same day if possible. This will ensure that they don't look elsewhere and leave you in the dust.

- Upon scheduling the appointment, let them know where the home is and when you will be there. Walk them through the home and comfortably try to answer any questions that they may have.

- Pick a time that you are not rushed so that you can take the time to answer questions. Unanswered questions are usually a deal breaker.

- Schedule a time that is suitable for them so they are not rushed as well. This will give them the opportunity to make a sound decision and you will potentially have a better resident if they know exactly what they are getting into.

It's Milkin' Time: Making Appointments

In our experience we have seen a lot of people come and go. The main thing that I can agree with is that they all want is a safe place to stay, convenience, a reasonable rate, and a quick response.

When you get a call, try to call back as soon as possible to ensure you get them while their need is very high. Next, make every means possible to get to show them the home quickly. Usually, their needs are immediate. You must act on that need very quickly. Then try to process the application quickly. Check their background, get a credit check, and try to get them approved right away. After doing a few of them, you will get the hang of it.

We usually have them make the appointment on the day they call us. If possible, have them view the home that same day or within a day or two. Then proceed with processing their application as quickly as possible. This will ensure that they can move in with very little time lapse.

There have been many times when we have had a call from a potential resident, made the appointment to meet and show the room within an hour or two, qualified them through a mobile online source, approved their application and gave them a key to move in the same day.

SHOWING THE HOME AND THE ROOM

HOW LONG SHOULD IT TAKE?

It can take you around a half an hour or more to show the room along with all the amenities the home has as well as answering any questions that they may have in order to feel comfortable about their decision. After showing the available rooms a few times, you will get better at reading what they are really looking for and gearing questions towards their needs *(like we have listed in the chapter "Making Appointments").*

SHOW THEM AROUND THE HOME

Show them where the kitchen is and where to find everything in it. Introduce them to anyone who is currently a resident there. Show them where the bathroom is and where they will potentially do their laundry. Show them the vacant room that is furnished with a bed and a dresser. Use this time to give them the confidence that this is a good place for them to stay that is safe, affordable, and convenient.

WHAT TO DO IF THEY ARE INTERESTED

If they are interested, you can then proceed to the application process. You can offer them an application form and tell them the application fee. You will want to wait to process the application until you have the complete processing fee in hand. This is a good time to let them know they can put money down to hold the room. They have to qualify to get the room before processing the deposit. Also let them know at this time what is required of the deposit and how to get their refundable deposit back.

We have three requirements that they have to complete before getting a deposit back.

1. The room has to be given back in good condition.

2. They have to return their room key.

3. They have to have all rent paid in full.

WHAT IF THEY ARE NOT INTERESTED?

If they are not interested, you will want to kindly thank them and offer your number to them to call if they need anything in the future. Don't be disappointed, it is not for everyone. However, keep a nice rapport with them in case they change their mind or their needs change further down the road. You may wind up meeting once again and working things in favor of both of you.

WHAT YOU NEED TO FILL THE ROOM

A COMPLETED APPLICATION AND PROCESSING FEE
You need an application form completed and processed. When you get the application, do a background check, run a credit report, and check their references. Check their background by looking into the references they have given you. Also check the judicial system to see if they have a felony charge which should deter you from wanting this resident in your home. Check their credit by going online through an agency that handles that for a minor fee. (You can collect this fee from the potential resident in the form of an "application and processing" fee.) After doing these a couple of times, it seems to be quite easy to tell if you have a potential resident that would qualify. What you charge is up to you. You will need to pay for the credit check, so you want to collect for that. The rest of the

total is paying yourself for your time you took to look up the information.

A QUALIFIED RESIDENT

What qualifies a resident is up to you. Look over their application and see if there are any red flags. Remember this is your home and they are going to live there so choose wisely. If they look like a reasonable person without a bad track record, they have money to put down for a deposit, an application and processing fee as well as money for a week's rent, they can turn out to be a likely resident. If they have a drug related past, have several things on their record, and don't have a plan for how they are coming up with the rent and deposit, they may not be a great choice.

PICTURE OF RESIDENT

Take a clear picture of their driver's license or photo identification card. If they do not have either, you can take their picture with a pocket digital camera. Store this on file with their application. Gather all this information while they are filling out the application.

A DEPOSIT TO HOLD THE ROOM

In most cases, you want to get the total of one week of rent to hold the room and call it a "deposit". This is money that you hold to refund them if they move out and the room is left in good condition, rent is paid in full and they give you back a key. If they do not do those things, you may choose to keep the deposit in order to compensate you for your trouble, time and finding a new resident.

THE FIRST WEEK'S RENT

Require that they pay a full week's rent after you approve them for residency and are serious about moving in. The second week they are staying require that they pay both the second week's rent plus any prorated rents from the first week. Let's say you set up to have all rent due on a Friday, if they move in on a Wednesday, you need to prorate Wednesday's and Thursday's rent for a partial week. If you wait until the second week to charge them the prorated rent, they don't get inundated with a bunch of expense at the beginning. This helps spread out the payments for them and you still get the cash.

PAYING AHEAD ON RENT
Although it should not be required, some people like to pay in advance if they are on a fixed income or if they do not want to bother paying weekly rent. You may want to offer for them to pay a monthly rent, as well as offer a discount when this occurs because you are getting paid in advance and have a guaranteed income for the weeks ahead.

STRATEGIES FOR FILLING ROOMS QUICKLY

TAKE YOUR TIME ANSWERING QUESTIONS

If you decide to manage your own property, find a time that you are not rushed when answering calls for potential residents and when showing rooms. Taking the time to answer questions carefully by listening to their needs can make or break getting a resident. Take that extra time at the beginning so they can be confident they are moving into a room and a home that is going to be suitable for them.

SHOW THEM AROUND

Show them more than one option if you have more than one room available. You want to give them enough time to ask questions and see what the home is like. Have a good idea of what the area is like around the home so you can let them know where things are, such as the local grocery store, restaurants, and the bus stop. Encourage them to look around the neighborhood. If there is parking available, let them know where it is if they have a vehicle.

BULK YOUR APPOINTMENTS TOGETHER

Another time-saving strategy that you should use is showing the room to more than one potential resident at a time. This does two things:

1. It saves you time running back and forth showing ten people the same property.

2. Gives the potential resident a feeling of competition which heightens your likelihood of filling the room. If someone wants the same thing that another person wants, sometimes it makes them want it even more. Bring a group in and take all their applications. Money talks, so when a potential resident has money to secure the room, you have something solid to work with. If you have several that qualify, pick the one with the best track record from their application process and try to reserve the other(s) to a waiting list for future vacancies.

How "in demand" are these rooms?

Don't worry--these rooms are needed and they do fill quickly. It can be very gratifying getting someone into a home whom otherwise had very little hope or idea of where they were going to live in the future. After having the home filled with tenants for a while and someone moves out, sometimes one person may have a friend that wants to move in right away. The word gets around quickly.

IT'S MILKIN' TIME: FILLING YOUR ROOM

We got a call from a guy one time that desperately needed a room. He said he was living in his car and he was home from the military. He had a big story of how his girlfriend had birthed his children and would not let him see them and he was trying to get custody. Naturally, we wanted to help this guy if what he said was the truth. I tried to make an appointment with him and he told me he would call back. He was on his cell phone.

He would call back a day or two later and he went on about the story but never made an appointment to see the room. He never had the money. I tried to direct him to some of the social services that work with us and that I thought they could help him in getting funding for his housing. He would always state he would call back.

This continued for a while. He went on with more of his story but would never get help for himself and would never make an appointment. We realized that there was no way for us to help him. This was a situation he must have wanted and he would work through it his own way.

To make sure we saved ourselves time, we tagged his number in our directory. When he called, we knew it was him and let it go to voicemail. Otherwise it would continue on a path that had no end. If he had left a message and mentioned an action plan, then we could have helped to service his needs. We could have then saved the time we spent trying to help others that needed our help and were willing to do what was needed to get that help.

Sometimes, although you may want to help someone so badly, some people do not want helped. They may just need to talk to someone. Listening may be the only service you provide them. It happens!

THE APPLICATION PROCESS

The Application Process

Where do you get applications?

You can get all of your forms including rental applications from the Landlord Protection Agency website: **http://www.thelpa.com** for a nominal yearly fee, you gain access to tons of information that you will find vital while renting to residents. You can order a credit report, get all kinds of questions answered and they offer excellent landlord support.

How does the potential tenant get an application?

You can make copies of applications and have them accessible to the potential tenant through either the mail or we give it to them when you meet with them at the property while the interest is high. Ask them to fill it out and submit it with the application fee for your review so you can get them approved as quickly as possible.

You may offer to meet them at a public place like a coffee shop. It offers a comfortable place to meet that has a nice atmosphere which is safe for new acquaintances to meet to fill out paperwork.

WHAT DO YOU DO WITH THE APPLICATION?

The application gives you plenty of useful information. You need their social security number to perform a credit check. Use their birthday, past and current addresses, and the correct and full name spelling to look them up on the ***Megan's Law List***. In certain states, you are not permitted to refuse anyone due to the Megan's law. That is when you can use the past credit history to look for unfavorable content to use to refuse, which is legal grounds for refusal to rent.

Have a digital picture of your residents so you have on file what each of your residents look like. You must also take a picture of their driver's license or picture identification card. You get their photo and useful information like their driver's license number.

BACKGROUND CHECK

Do a background check on everyone. Don't neglect to look at where they have lived previously, past work, and references taken from an application. This is going to give you a great idea of what kind of person they are and have been in the past.

CREDIT CHECK

Credit checks don't take very long and don't cost much. There are many resources online that provide the ability to do a credit check with the correct amount of information such as a full name, birth date, and social security number. Inform your resident that you are going to do a credit check on them. A credit report can give you valuable information as to whether or not they may be a good paying resident. They may have poor credit, but you can still house them anyway. What you are looking for is inexcusable behavior such as not paying past rent to a previous landlord.

CRIMINAL BACKGROUND RESEARCH

Due to the fact that you might be housing more than one resident per home and you want to keep a peaceful community, please use discretion and take the time to look over each potential resident. Criminals are to be taken very seriously while there are other residents in these homes that you are providing the best housing possible for. Do a criminal search in the state they live in and any past areas as well. Don't forget to check Megan's law in those areas too.

THE SUPER-TENANT

The Super-Tenant

What is a super-tenant?

This person is someone who you bring in as a resident who helps you manage your other residents and the property. A super-tenant lives in one of the rooms either rent free or for partial-rent. In lieu of the rent, this person has a few responsibilities that the other residents do not. They may include but are not limited to:

- Cleaning the common areas once a week

- Handling any maintenance issues that come up

- Mowing the grass or shoveling the walkway of snow

- Taking the garbage out once a week on pick-up night

- Showing available rooms for you

- Taking care of any issues that may arise with the other residents

A super-tenant is an excellent strategy for the homeowner who does not want to be a landlord.

HOW DO YOU FIND A SUPER-TENANT?
By placing an ad in the local paper you may find this type of resident. Some people are very handy and very good at dealing with people. You are also helping them out by offering them a place to stay. They are helping you out by taking care of those landlord responsibilities that you may not really care to do. "Free room for rent for someone willing to help with home maintenance, taking care of managing other residents in home, and some minor cleaning. Please call xxx-xxx-xxxx or email xxxxxxxx.com"

If you already have residents, you may want to offer the "position" to one that you find trustworthy.

HOW DO YOU COMPENSATE A SUPER-TENANT?

Like always, you can use your own discretion. You can offer them a discounted rent or offer them free rent.

Now That You Have a Qualified Resident, What is Next?

NOW YOU HAVE A QUALIFIED RESIDENT. WHAT IS NEXT?

LET THEM KNOW THEY ARE APPROVED TO MOVE IN

Let the resident know you have processed their application and they are approved to be a resident. You can set up a time to meet with them to give them a key to their room, a copy of the house rules, and welcome them into their new place.

WHAT YOU SHOULD LET THEM KNOW UP FRONT

Here is a list of things you want to let your new resident know at this time:

You will not be responsible for anything that the tenant brings in because they have a lock and key to their room that they can store all of their goods in.

Let them know that they may want to get renter's insurance. This will take care of any loss they may incur while being a renter toward any of their own personal items in case of a fire or other damages that renter's insurance covers.

Let them know that they need to bring their own linens and toiletry items.

GIVE THEM A RECEIPT FOR PAYMENT
Give them a statement or receipt of what they have already paid and let them know that their rent is covered up until the next rent due day. Also let them know what will be due at that time and every week after just to reiterate what has already been discussed. Give them a receipt EVERYTIME they hand you a payment.

STATEMENT OF ACCOUNT
Give them a statement of account every week to help them keep track of their account of what is owed and what has been paid.

Congratulations! You can now start to enjoy the benefits of rental property with a paying resident.

What do new residents need from you?

Now that you have a qualified resident, what do they need from you in order to get moved in? There are certain forms that you should give to everyone who moves in.

A copy of the house rules

This is a list of all the rules that every person must abide by in order to reside in the house. If they do not obey these rules, you will usually hear about it from another resident or a neighbor. Just try to deal with each issue as it comes and handle it accordingly. Set up house rules for their safety and for a peaceful environment. Let them know that if they break these rules you will notify them with a rules violation. Take the time to go over the rules with them to see if they have any questions.

A KEY FOR THEIR ROOM

Give each resident a key for their room and make sure you have a spare in case you do not get it back. Let them know if they lock themselves out of their room, you will charge them a fee to come and unlock the door.

KEY CODE FOR THE FRONT DOOR

If you decided to put a digital lock on the entry door, you need to program each new resident with a code of their own that should be easy for them to remember. Don't forget to record the code in their file if you ever need to change it or if the resident forgets. For everyone's safety, do not give this code to anyone and let the resident know that they should not either.

MONTH TO MONTH VERBAL LEASE AGREEMENT

Because people may come and go quickly you want to stick with a month to month verbal lease. Just stress to the resident at this time that in order get their deposit back, they do need to give you a one-week notice. Also indicate that the verbal lease consists of following the house rules.

SETTING UP PROPER COMMUNICATIONS

EMERGENCY NUMBERS

You want to post the neighborhood emergency numbers for your residents to call places like 911, the police, the fire department, and things of that nature. Have these numbers readily available and easy to read near the land-line phone of the home.

HOW WILL YOUR RESIDENT CONTACT YOU?

Not only do you want to provide a number for them to call you in the event of an emergency, but a mailing address too. You may not want this to be your personal residence or personal cell phone, but you need to provide them with a way to reach you in an emergency. You can provide a post office box for them to mail their rent to you. You may also want to consider putting in a **lock-box** at the home for all residents to place their rent. They may have paperwork that you need to fill out that helps them get assistance toward their rent. Having a common area that you check often, that is secured, can be very timely and efficient.

HOW WILL YOU CONTACT YOUR RESIDENT?
Make sure you have a number to reach your resident as soon as they move in. As you speak with your resident from time to time, make sure that number has not changed. Also realize if you decide to put in a land line phone, you should be able to reach each resident or have a message delivered in order to get a hold of someone. If you need to send paperwork, ask them if they have a post office box or how they want to receive mail. This way, they know something is on its way and they should look for it to be received. Keep this communication open because there can be

nothing more frustrating than trying to reach someone to no availability.

PROVIDING A LAND LINE PHONE

This is an affordable way to get new residents and to keep the ones you have happy. It is so nice for them to have a line they can use at any time. If you provide this for your residents, make sure to work with the phone company to block certain types of toll calls going out. Make sure your provider is able to make an adjustment that only local and long-distance is provided for a monthly fee with no pay per view allowed or toll calls out of the country without a calling card.

Managing your Property

Making sure the property is properly maintained

Do it yourself or hire help

 Now that you have residents living in your home, you want to make sure that you maintain the property so that everything runs efficiently. You don't have to do this yourself. You can hire someone to do regular maintenance visits on the home or you can find a "Super-Tenant" as explained in the section on "Filling your property with residents". These are some creative ways you can maintain the property. You may also want to just check up on things and do maintenance yourself. This will also save you money by doing it yourself.

How do you know what needs to be done?

Sometimes the residents will let you know when something is in need of repair. They pay you rent in order to have a home in working order so it is a good thing to keep up with all of the repairs, mowing, any yard work, sidewalk shoveling, and things of that nature. A properly maintained home will keep your residents happy and content. You may also want to schedule maintenance visits occasionally.

CLEANING THE COMMON AREAS

CLEANING THE COMMON AREA

Everyone is to take care of their own room, but there is still the area that everyone shares that you need to consider. Right from the start, let the residents each know that they are expected to pick up after themselves. That includes the bathroom, living room, and the kitchen area.

Just for good measure, you may want to consider having someone come in once a week to sweep, mop, vacuum, and wipe down the common areas. Whether this is you or someone you hire to do it, it helps do several things:

- It keeps the home clean overall. It is hard to decide who sweeps, who mops, that sort of thing; so as a service, have someone handle that once a week.

- It also helps you keep an eye on your residents. If there are problems with someone not keeping up with their share of the cleanup, a regular conversation with the residents will soon help you find your culprit. It doesn't take long for the residents to build a relationship with one another and the person that is cleaning the house. Pretty soon you have all the information you need to find out who the resident may be that is causing problems in the house.

- It is easier to monitor any abuse going on such as someone leaving a window open while you are heating the house or who is leaving the laundry in the washing machine or dryer undone. What you do is send them a written warning. If it is found again, they get a rules violation.

SUGGESTIONS ON THE COST OF CLEANING

Having someone keep the place clean can be very affordable and can be paid for by the residents through their rent. Pay someone an hourly rate to clean the kitchen, bathroom, living room, and entry area (otherwise referred to as "the common areas") as well as picking up around the outside. This generally takes about one hour to an hour and a half as long as they are not cleaning up a big mess after someone. If they do, give a rules violation to that person who is responsible and that money in turn is used to pay for the additional cleaning. Find someone who will bring their own cleaning supplies so you do not have to supply these items.

ITS MILKING TIME: CLEANING PERSONNEL

Once, the cleaning personnel showed up to a yard full of garbage. It was everywhere! It took her an hour and a half to clean the mess which we had to pay for. Luckily she had the time available to work over, but what we discovered was that we needed a new system set up for garbage disposal.

The residents were putting the garbage out, but they were using cheap bags and setting it out whenever the bag was full. Some of the bags may have been out for several days up to a week. The local pesky neighborhood critters were getting into it and had it all over the place. The city will fine you for a mess like that.

What we decided to do is buy the big industrial size bags as well as two large and tall kitchen garbage cans with handles on either side. As the cleaning person goes into the home to clean, they change out the bags which are very full by a week's time.

She puts them out at the curb on the designated evening. She also takes extra bags and puts them on the garbage can handles so that if the garbage does fill up, they have an accessible bag and change it out. She cleans the home strategically on the day before the garbage is due and sets it out. It has absolved this issue.

Maintain Good Records

Good Record Keeping

To be able to keep track of payments coming in and payments going out, it is a good idea to have some system of keeping records. You can find a bookkeeper to handle the day-to-day transactions for your home that you rent out, or you can choose to do it yourself.

It is important to keep consistent records no matter how you decide to put them down on paper or on a computer program. This will help you know exactly how much you are making every month. It will also help you see if you have too much of an expense going out in one area or not enough coming in from a resident.

You will also need these records when it is time to do your taxes every year.

MONITOR UTILITY ABUSE

HEATING
Heating cost can be lowered by having an efficiency heater installed. Have the thermostat set at round 70 degrees and have a **lock-box** on it. These boxes are excellent and can be found at home improvement stores. Set up the budget plan with the utility company so you will know approximately what your total will be every month.

CENTRAL AIR OR AIR CONDITIONERS
If the home has central air, then you can monitor it at the thermostat, but cover it with a lock-box.

WATER USAGE
Keep an eye on the water bill. If it goes up, find out why. If there a leaky toilet, fix it. Is someone letting a friend do laundry? If so, it is a *rules violation* and you need to give

them a written notice. Let them know if it happens again it is grounds for eviction.

If you don't know who is doing it, ask the residents. It is a community and they will work together or against each other to keep their own costs down. If you tell them that you are all getting assessed a dollar a week more until it is found out who it is, they will more than likely spill the beans on who is causing the rules violation.

IT'S MILKIN' TIME: UTILITY ABUSE

One month our water bill went up by three times more than normal! When we went in to assess the problem, we discovered that someone turned on the basement sink and just left it running. It may have been running for the entire month. Now we have our weekly cleaning personnel check all over the house for any potential abuse and we have our maintenance manager completely shut off any water sources that are not viable to just survival (basement water sources and outdoor spigots).

Another time, we learned that one resident was letting his friends come in and do their laundry. We do not pay the water bill so some guy can bring anyone in to do their laundry. This is against the rules and we sent him a violation. He understood that if it happened again, it would cost him the price of having a place to live.

Immediately upon finding out, we spoke with him and let him know that this is something we had learned and that it is not permitted. We also told him we were sending him a violation. It is important to not only communicate it to the resident in violation, but to also do something about it so it doesn't happen again.

We then reviewed our house rule for the violation and how it was written to make sure that the rule the resident was breaking was clear. It stated in our rules violations that the in-house laundry facility was in fact only for the residents who live in the home. If we found that the language did not state this clearly, this would be a good time to re-word that statement so that there was no mistake with a resident understanding exactly what was included in that rule.

It may seem like it makes sense to just anyone that you don't leave water running in a basement or that you don't let your friends do their laundry in the home you rent a room at. It may not be the language and how it is written. It may just be that someone wants to try to see what they can get away with.

Managing Your Residents

KEEPING YOUR RESIDENTS LIVING IN YOUR HOME

To ensure that you not only pay the bills of the home but also maintain a profit, you want to keep each of the rooms filled with a resident.

CREATE A GOOD ENVIRONMENT

By making the home a good, healthy environment in which to live, you may not have to be concerned about residents wanting to move out. Be proactive by keeping the home clean, maintaining good communication with the residents, offering what is needed and you will have much better luck keeping the residents that you do have.

BE PREPARED WHEN VACANCY ARISES

If you learn that you are about to have a vacancy start the system for getting a new resident. By the time a resident is moving out, you can have someone else ready to view the room and possibly move in right away.

CREATIVE ATTENTION TO RESIDENTS

By occasionally doing something special for your residents, it may be the very reason they do not ever want to move. How nice would it be if you sent a pizza for everyone to enjoy. You don't have to do things like this but they will remember if you do. Perhaps drop off a couple of dozen cookies for everyone to devour. It can be an affordable way to do something out of the ordinary and maintain a great relationship with those in your home. It may also add something to the community of people you have living there and how they get along.

KEEP PROPERTY MAINTAINED PROPERLY

By keeping up with all maintenance of the home, you will keep a much happier resident. Much happier residents don't want to move out. If you do not want to do the maintenance, you can hire a helping hand or look up the section on "Super-Tenant" and learn ways of maintaining the property without having to do the work yourself.

SCREEN POTENTIAL RESIDENTS WELL

By choosing your residents well, you may have a much more manageable person living in your home. When they are more manageable, they will get along much better with you and other residents, potentially pay their rent on time, and communicate well with you when potential issues arise.

Moving a Resident Out

Receive a Notice to Move Out

Any resident that wants to move out AND receive their security deposit back that they put down on the room should leave you with a one-week written or verbal notice. If they move out with no notice, you do not have to refund the deposit. If they do give you notice, this gives you ample time to get a new resident. You will soon recover that deposit plus a new resident in no time, having a week to do so.

Criteria for Refunding a Deposit

Let your residents know you can refund the deposit when they give you back a key, they have all rent paid in full and the room is left in good condition as per your *exit inspection*.

Refunding a Deposit

After the resident is moved out, left the room in good condition, returned the key, rent is paid in full, and already given their one week notice, you can make arrangements to refund their cash deposit.

When Not to Refund a Deposit

In the case where the tenant is moved out because of a rules violation or unpaid rent, you can apply their security deposit towards any damages incurred to the property due to a rules violation or their moving out. Keep in mind the term "damages" does not only apply to physical damages, but can also be applied to unpaid rent or a "damaged" lease.

Physical removal of a resident and their property

In the event that you need to evict a resident, every state will have different laws. Find out what laws you need to abide by in order to properly evict a resident.

Creative evictions

Some people that need to move out due to a rules violation or a broken lease are not very willing to go. One way is to offer them $x.xx to move out in 24 hours. They need the money to move on and it will save you quite a bit in eviction fees.

If there is no lease in place, give them a 24-hour lockout notice. Change out the locks and pack their things storing them for up to an extended period of time (2-3 weeks). They will have to contact you in order to receive their belongings in which you can make arrangements to do so.

It's Milkin Time: Security Deposit

When we first started renting out rooms, we had cases where we would give back partial deposits. We always try to be fair to everyone because their money is so hard to come by.

There was a particular occasion where we reserved $35.00 of the deposit to repair a hole and refunded the rest. That was early on and we have learned to no longer give out partial deposits. It is too difficult to figure out exactly what the expenses will be on any particular damage and they are usually long gone when the damage is being repaired.

They either earned back the total deposit by what we require or they are forfeit their deposit from some form of neglect to the agreement. It is much easier to follow one system that everyone follows than to make a particular case very every single person that comes along. Follow your systems and keep them in place by being consistent.

LOCKING OUT A RESIDENT

24-HOUR LOCKOUT NOTICE

This is a notice that you give a resident after they have not paid their rent on time. The reason you want to do this is because getting behind on rent can add up very quickly. You can deliver notices as soon as the resident is officially late. If you have rent due on a Friday, and by Monday morning you haven't received rent, you want to post a 24-hour lockout notice. This gives the resident the heads up that they will be locked out of their home and the room until they are paid up or you move in another resident. At that time, they have to go through the entire process again. Keep in mind, you may find a good example of a 24-hour lockout notice on LPA.com.

DELETING THE KEY CODE TO MAIN ENTRY

After the 24-hour notice has expired, if your resident has not contacted you and made a plan to get paid in full, you should honor the notice and delete the resident's code to the front door. When they can't get in, they will either call you or make arrangements somehow to get their things.

CHANGE OUT THE LANDLORD LOCKS

You should also change out the landlord locks. They may still be able to enter the house via another resident. That is fine and you should not involve the other residents in the locking out of a previous resident (unless they are the Super-Tenant). The landlord locks are designed so that anyone with a master key can remove the lock cylinder from the door knob in seconds which can then be exchanged for a different lock. If the resident wants to get their belongings or be able to get to move back in, they will need to contact you immediately. Keep in mind, once a resident is locked out; you need to make arrangements to move them out. If they do not contact you soon after the lockout, make arrangements to pack their things and store them for an extended period of time. This is your home and they are considered to be trespassing if they have no entry into the home. You need to change those locks. Also, now that you have a vacancy, you want to start looking for a new resident.

Rules Violations and House Rules

What are rules violations?

In the home it is recommended that you have a set of house rules that everyone living there needs to follow in order to keep harmony within the household. *Rules violations* are given in written form to a resident or residents when one or more of your residents break one or more of your house rules at your property. After discussing the rule that has been violated, you need to give them written notice that they broke this rule and charge a fee for the violation.

Rules violations are like a lesson for children. You need to discipline them the moment you see the issue. Don't wait a week and then slap their hand. They will forget what they have done. By next week they may have another rules violation and you may need to charge them again with another fee. When you take immediate action, you are protecting your home. Be flexible, but you do not want them messing up your property, wreaking havoc on the home, or bringing in unfavorable conditions.

WHAT ARE HOUSE RULES?

When a potential tenant signs up for a room, you should give them a list of "House Rules" that you expect they follow. These rules should also be posted in the common areas for everyone to see. Some of these rules contain wording for things like; no pets, one person living per bedroom, clean up after yourself, no garbage thrown about the yard, etc. The Landlord Protection Agency may have information on rules that will help you create your own "house rules" that you find fitting for your room-for-rent environment.

It's Milkin' Time: Rules Violations

Once, we had a tenant that was giving us a difficult time. They were always trying to push it. We found out that they were having friends in until the wee hours, staying up late and being loud. We gave them a rules violation and stated that that behavior was unacceptable for a home that was shared.

They got mad and decided that they would move out. They were sure they would find something better. Well, that was great and we wished them the best of luck.

We got a call a few weeks later from the previous resident asking to come back. Even though we did not evict this person, we did not have to move them back in. We let them know that they were too hard to live with for the other residents and their behavior was unacceptable. They were not an ideal resident for the type of rental property we were providing.

If you find that someone is not working out for your rental property, it is your responsibility to make sure you handle it. Giving the perfect home and environment is not possible, but finding a peaceful solution can be possible and should try to be obtained.

Other Policies to Consider While Renting Out Rooms

OTHER POLICIES TO CONSIDER WHEN RENTING TO RESIDENTS

BEING RESPONSIBLE FOR TENANT'S PROPERTY

We are not responsible for anything that the tenant brings in because they have a lock and key to their room that they can store all of their things in. We let them know in the application process that they need to bring their own linens and toiletry items. We let them know that we provide a bed and a dresser for their use, a lock and key entry into their room, a shared kitchen, shared bathroom and shared living space. We let them know also that they can bring their own dorm fridge to store in their rooms for their own food.

SUGGEST A RENTER'S INSURANCE POLICY PER RESIDENT

A renter's insurance policy will help cover a resident's belongings in the event that anything would be destroyed.

Smoking Policy for Residents

We do permit smoking because a majority of our tenants are smokers. There is nothing in our insurance policy that states otherwise, so we permit it to cater to our tenants.

Linens and Reusable Items

We do not provide linens or reusable products for tenants. That is stressed in the application process. We do pay to have someone come in and clean the "Common Areas" once a week. The "Common Area" is all of the areas that all tenants have access to, including the entry, kitchen, bathroom/s, and living room space. At that time, they stock the bathroom with toilet paper for everyone to use.

GLOSSARY

Glossary

Eviction: When a resident is forced to move because they have failed to pay rent or have gone against the rules of the place in which they are paying rent. There is a formal process to go through an eviction. They can be timely, but are necessary in order to get a paying resident back in the home that you rent out.

Exit Inspection: This is a general inspection carried out by the property manager or homeowner when a resident is about to move out or has moved out. You may want to check for damage, items left behind, and any missing items that you provide for your residents (beds, dressers, etc.).

Forfeit: To give up something. In this case, we were referring to a resident giving up their deposit to redeem a fine or unpaid rent.

House rules: Rules that are set and posted within your rental home for all residents to abide by.

Lock-box: A box that you can mount on a solid surface that has a lock and key. There is a place on the box for small items to be placed that cannot be retrieved without a key. A lock-box is great for receiving envelopes with rent payment or dropping off a key for a landlord.

Monthly statement: A written statement that you can create and give to your resident once a month just before rent is due that explains what is owed.

Non-Payer Lockout: This is a term that describes the action of locking out a resident that has not paid you after you have given them a written notice. After receiving this and they don't pay, you change out the locks so when they return they cannot enter causing a non-payer lockout.

Rules violations are when a resident break rules at your property and you give them a notice that they broke this rule and are receiving a fine for the violation.

Security Deposits: The money a potential resident gives a landlord in order to "Secure" or hold the property.

Statement of account is a written record of what is owed by a customer. A statement for a rental may include totals such as rent, deposit, service fees, late fees, rules violations, processing fees, and application fees.

Tenant: Someone that lives in a living environment that is rented from a landlord. They may also be referred to as "Resident".

Vacancy: When a property is not lived in; an unoccupied space. Something a landlord does not want. When you fill any rental with a resident, it is no longer vacant.

Vouchers: Vouchers act like a guarantee that you will get money from a particular organization. Generally, it may take a few weeks to get the money, but when you get the commitment from a voucher it is as good as cash in the bank once received.

Wait List: A list of people's names and numbers that you put together in order that they called who want a room for rent but were not able to take a room at the time they originally called for one reason or another. You can use this list to get residents for any vacancy that may occur.

INDEX

24-hour lockout notice, 111

application form, 52

background check, 52, 67

cable television, 24
checks, 67
converting rooms, 19
credit check, 52
criminal search, 68

deposit, 42

eviction, 108, 125
exit inspection, 125

false walls, 20

helping the community, 36
house rules, 21, 80, 115, 126

internet, 24

keeping records, 96

key codes
    assigning, 23

land-line phone, 25
Landlord Protection
    Agency, 65, 115
laundry, 27
linens, 122
lock-box, 126

maintenance visits, 89
Megan's law, 66
monthly statement, 126

neighborhood, 57
non-payer lockout, 126

pets, 43
photo identification, 53
placing ads, 35
processing fee, 50

questions, 41

references, 52
refunding a deposit, 106
renter's insurance, 121
room requirements, 20

rules violations, 98, 114, 127

secure lock and key entry, 20
security deposits, 127
shelters, 40
smoking, 122
statement of account, 127
super-tenant, 71

tenant, 127

utilities, 24
utility abuse, 98

vacancy, 128
verbal lease, 82
vouchers, 128

waiting list, 128
water, 26
word of mouth, 36

www.ingramcontent.com/pod-product-compliance
Lightning Source LLC
Chambersburg PA
CBHW030809180526
45163CB00003B/1209